It Doesn't Matter What You Want

David Mac

ISBN: 978-81-19654-51-2

First Edition: 2024
Rs. 200/-

Cyberwit.net
HIG 45 Kaushambi Kunj, Kalindipuram
Allahabad - 211011 (U.P.) India
http://www.cyberwit.net
Tel: +(91) 9415091004
E-mail: info@cyberwit.net

Printed at Repro India Limited.

Contents

In Tokyo 7
Mornings without You 8
The Impression I Get Or Do Not Get 10
And Love Flows Like Mud 11
From my Chair 13
Pill Girl 14
After Lorca 16
For You, Babe 17
The Agony of the Flame 19
Daddy's Girl 20
Wine Drenched 21
Mascara 22
News 23
Black Night Thing 24
The Cunt is a Cunt 25
Somewhere the Sun 26
Sharp 28
Basic Thing 29
Buildings and Rooms 30
Revolutions 31
Tempo 32
9-5 33
Red Beat 34
Smash The Bottle, It's Morning 35
Parlour Thoughts 37
Experiments with Gravity 39
Something Fishy About Today 40
Morning Horny 41
Only Half 42

The Sleeper 43
Love Story 44
Square as Hell 45
And the Birds Burn into the Sun 46
Poem You 47
The Bluest Blues 48
Send these Poems to Hell 49
Our Poems 50
Stirring Through Thoughts That Mean Absolutely Nothing 52
Black Wine 54
You are not Humphrey Bogart, and you'll never get over it 55
K.O.C. 57
Pollock 58
Your Red 59
Ask My Dick 61
The End of a Love 62
Interrogation whilst eating a Cherry in the World 63
You've Been Back Here, I Can Tell 64
Varnish 65
Indentation of Something 66
I am eating an apple 68
This Sober Thing 69
Do Another Day 70
For You, Babe 72
Boil 74
Vow 75
As I Do My Best 76
Forming 78
Through Walls 80
Love Is Just Another Arsehole 81
Try This 83

In Tokyo

The TV was on: some futuristic samurai film, a car chase.
I'd taken a pill and danced by the lamp for ages;
it made the shadows excited and go crazy.
She smoked her tinfoil on the sofa and said
slowly, 'Them Japanese make mad movies!'
I nodded and gulped, saw the Tokyo skyline,
gulped and rushed. She closed her eyes and I felt
my heart shudder. So I stood still finally, for a
moment. The shadows stood too.
We all watched her. We all stood.
Which is where I stand now, remembering.
Shit, what was the name of that fucking movie?

Mornings without You

Mornings are the worst.
Kids and animals don't see this yet
but I know it.

You're responsible for hurting my life, for
breaking my world, for
desecrating my happiness.

Leave your dust and pretty ornaments. Leave
your lipstick marks and fingerprints. Leave
your cigarette butts and sweet perfume.
Leave my love by the door.
Leave my heart on the floor.

The world is hanging on the broom.
I swept up the teardrops.

If I dream, do you smile?
If I take that smile and
give you this dream…
Keep it, it's yours.

If it falls, let it fall.

But I been banging on back-streets,
going back to the start,
and there's death all day long
whichever way you look at things.

What's the point in today?
You're a ghost and I'm
stirring my poems with a spoon.

It's okay.

I wrote it all down this morning
so I wouldn't forget it,
so I wouldn't forget you
and your name

in this place.

The Impression I Get Or Do Not Get

We flicker like candles
our smiles like moths seeking the next suicide

Your eyes become used teabags
my voice becomes a scratched record

This is what we do
This is our procedure

Outside there are red women walking into the falling sun
dreaming of hard men to echo between their thighs

and I am skinned forever, looking at everything
a hungry eye, seeing things turn and snarl

You want to get a taxi and head out across town
claim a little piece of the night

I tell you that I wish it would be a yellow one
like out of a NYC motion picture, and

I don't want to ever go out and be with people
it's not my fault the world smells of semen

I want to be Renoir, Monet, Degas
I want to be Cezanne

I want to see colours for the first time

And Love Flows Like Mud

She lay there
All that meat
All that flesh

He shuts the door
Lets his skin fall to the floor

He comes to the hot bed
His dick a mad wolf
Screaming and angry

Spiking her
She throbs and writhes
A pink fish speared

Her black eyes ooze
His tongue flicks
Wriggles into her mouth
A violent worm

They twist and jerk
Wild patterns
But her beauty dances

He juts
Splits
Shoots off into darkness

Bodies collapse
Break apart

And after
They smoke cigarettes
Strangers again

No words

Will her cock remember?
Will his cunt forget?

From my Chair

Staring into space really doesn't hurt anyone.
My feet on the floor, my hands on my lap,
head cloudless, mind see-through,
contemplating big bit of nothing
on the wall from my chair.
Last night in my dream
I was queuing for ice cream.
What's this mean?
That my thoughts are soft whipped,
thick white smooth,
cold dollop scoop,
in a cone,
with a flake on top,
that's what!
But now awake and reposed,
vacant, blank, far far away.
What do you expect me to do?
Dance or something?
No chance!

Pill Girl

And her eyes,
exploding into blackholes,
sucking everything inwards.
Her perverse smile,
we her children,
laughing,
playing,
redfaced and
mad.
The dirty sun,
wrung out,
dripping in a desolate sky,
buildings quivering,
undulating,
trembling up
above us.
And she screams,
burns like glue,
as cars pass,
shuffle,
cars with people,
humans, things,
creatures, meat,
heads, faces, minds,
stuffed full of milky souls that
exit out the back of their necks.
Then car wrecks,
collisions,
crashes,

bent and buckled metal,
shattering windscreens.
The town grins,
eats us whole.
But she is
high as birds,
half moon half mirror,
the hurtful planet curling to her song,
her oozing note,
and we all hear it
booming up to our bony homes,
our ragged lives,
and we clap and go
wild.
Stomp!
This night is ours.

After Lorca

I will sip orange until she finds me
I will only play with cats

I will hang my thoughts in the bare winter trees
I won't laugh like birds

But I will wait through these hard ages
I will curl up to the sky

For while she is gone
I will hurt like stone

For You, Babe

The days burn
almost as much
as the nights
ever did
and yes you're still a
blonde maniac

but your tits are good
and your arse is good
and your pussy is
very good

and I love that
small roll of fat
over your jeans
or the way you
spit out your gum or
smoke half a cigarette
or belch
just like a man

It's these little things that
numb the heavy burn
that almost heal
this pain

like it's only temporary
of course

like you
like me
like this

moment
right now

going
out

of our minds

The Agony of the Flame

This night is like
Any night
But a candle knows best
And flickers
Dancing its own volition

I guess I'm lonely
Like the moth
I'm too intrigued
The darkness lingers
But it is not enough

I have come here to burn
You look at me
Your face the
Only thing I see

You smile
I smile back

But in the blackness
What difference does it make?

Daddy's Girl

I'd hate to have a daughter
To watch your little girl grow
up and know she's
out there being
bad and getting
fucked
by men, like
you were, like
you are, and
maybe in the
back of
        c a r s

Wine Drenched

Wine drenched
Sky red
The angels coming through stained

And you look like
Death warmed up
A readymeal from the microwave

Your face harbours
Ugly expressions
Slicing all the angels in the room

No wonder
They have to leave
You're sober, and that's why I fucking hate you

Mascara

beetles in your boudoir belch from your black liquid eyes
your heart's a grey ashtray the shape of a skull

I have come here again with my bouquet of wilting flowers
I have come to lovingly break your neck

and you can hardly believe the words hissing from my mouthpiece
they are not the ones you expected

so, as I cross the room to find a vase, all that separates us is
the sound of tears from your eyes, and poison from mine

News

There is a heavy shower, there is a murder
A woman buying chips, a man getting stabbed in the face
They are the same thing, in the end

There is lunacy in paper headlines
Black ink, bloodshot eyes
On and on and on this history stretches

Coins travel from saints to madmen
Shops are big rooms that try to sell everything
I am hollow and intrusive
I need to know what I can before it's too late

A can in the gutter, a crushed cigarette under the heel
The rain is expected to last
The murderer will never be caught and will kill again and again
Superstardom is the meaning of life

If you look you can see no colour
So get out of your black head

News doesn't bother me
Everyone is doing the exact same thing

Black Night Thing

This black night
is like any other
time of day,
it's how you handle it
that matters.
This black night,
it's what you do with it
that counts,
what you do *to* it
that goes all the way:
how you learn,
how you shake,
how you remember
the daylight,
how you take in
all that blackness,
as if it's madness,
and for a moment
you're not so lost,
like you're
right there
and the darkness just
screams out.

The Cunt is a Cunt

The cunt never stops
it don't shut up

The cunt keeps on
screaming in my mind

The cunt keeps snarling
from between thighs

it keeps whispering
beneath dresses

The cunt is rude and angry
all day long

It mocks and laughs and
hisses my name

It coughs and spits and
belches and swears

It needs to be fed to
make it smile

Yep, the cunt plays
on my mind

But I should learn to
stand up to bullies

Somewhere the Sun

Somewhere along the way
The gods ended and
The madmen took over everything

Somewhere along the way
The poets leapt like tigers
Or wanted to

And the clock faces smiled and
The darkness was unexplainable
And the blues crept in
When your back was turned

But it's no problem
Only the sun knows
What's on the other side

The trick is to hammer it out
True
To let it all fall away

The trick is to never know
To feel it raw
Opening out around you
Like there's nothing left to lose

The trick is to get it down
On the line
Just right

And not to worry

In time you'll make it through
And it will be good

In time you'll turn everything
Into words

Sharp

When the booze screams your name
like it knows you
and the madmen are no longer on fire

When the gods begin to make sense
and death turns away coz he's
seen your face before

you got troubles, brother
like only the sky knows

Basic Thing

The poem is just like everything else:
you eat
you drink
you breathe
you shit
you make love
(if you're lucky)

you live and you die

It's vital, essential
instinctive
necessary
and beyond that too

It's basic in its element
this thing

how it comes, how
it flows through
no questions asked

You write the poem as you live your life
You live your life as you write the poem

If you want to stop, well
that's up to you

Buildings and Rooms

'I don't drive'
she said
'I don't wanna ever get
that far away'

And she hung a
dark shawl
over the window
and only patches
of sunlight
stabbed through
the holes

And outside
in the town
there were buildings
and rooms
some of which I had been in
some of which I had not

and the people
the people moved about the place
coz that's what
people do

Revolutions

Cleaning the house is pointless
Mowing the lawn is pointless
Washing the car is pointless

The planet turns
Life goes on
The 92 elements
From a dying star

This universe is stretching
Outwards

So I close my eyes
Sip my wine
And try

To remember her face

Tempo

I've been tapping a beer can
to BB King
for eternity
now
and you've been
screaming for days
weeks
hollow seasons.
At night
so as not to wake you
I piss into
empty wine bottles.
In the morning
I pluck words off
the ceiling
and
ignore you again.
This will go on
forever
or
it will not.

9-5

The everyday terror of trying to live
The hard true line scrawled across the page
The sky's a fool and it knows it

People on the planet under the sun
People in grey buildings 9-5
The way the girl's eyes locate me

But the bar don't open for another couple of hours
So what do you want to do?

Red Beat

Your heart is a big red bell,
a pumping howl,
a hot steamy pie,
and so is mine.
They keep their legendary ticking,
their sore beat
like the glad voice of God.
Listen…
We are alive, we are in love,
the pulse is fierce.
Do you hear?
Listen…
Our hearts' clock is
the only time that matters.

Smash The Bottle, It's Morning

When she woke up next to me she used to smile a lot.
She'd yawn and stretch and blink and then do that
crazy fucking smile.
She'd leap up and open the curtains and look at the new day.
I looked at her jiggling little arse.

'Isn't it a lovely-looking day?' she said.
She breathed in, out, looked at everything,
excited like a little kid.
'I love that first moment in the fresh new morning. A new day.
So happy!'

I groaned and moaned and shook.
My stomach turned with dread.
Here I was,
I had survived for another day.
I was here, still alive.

She talked and I just stared at the empty wine bottle by the bed.
Ah, this song of life, taunting me.
My head hurt,
I covered my ears.

That empty bottle,
I thought about just smashing it,
shattering it to pieces,
and then
stabbing
and

cutting
and bleeding myself
with
the
jagged shards.

Parlour Thoughts

She bends over to reveal her pussy:
pink, fleshy, almost luxuriant.
She says 'You like?'
but I'm indifferent.

I look at it and wonder
what it means.
To a man this is the world opened up,
like a flower, hot and mad,
but my mind's still on
a poem I have
not yet written.

Yes, what if I were to fuck her
with a poem?
What if I were to stick
a big hard poem up there?
Would she prefer a poem
to a cock?
Would it change her?

I stand mesmerised
by her thing,
smiling, having
my delicious thoughts,
and she stands up
and says:
'You're a poet aren't ya?'

I nod.

'I knew it. You were
thinking about
sticking a poem up there
weren't ya?'

I nod.

'Shit, you fucking lot
are all the same!'

Experiments with Gravity

When I was 8 I pushed a cat out of the upstairs window.
It landed on its feet.
The same day I pushed my grandmother out the same window.
She went to hospital.
I have always been a scientist.

Something Fishy About Today

Dead fish floating on the surface of the sky,
your smile is like a red bag of nails,
your heart is black mud,
your skin – cool as glass.
Bubbles fizz in my bottle, they
measure time,
the time in which we
don't say a word.
This silence can kill but
there's no such thing as silence anyhow.
Deep down I want my ideas to eat you.
Deep down I want to say something complex,
profound, something that'll
make your eyes shine like crystals
and not them
dirty old pennies.
Here, rattle your thoughts and drink up.
The sun's coming out and
I want to see
what it looks like.

Morning Horny

You wake up so horny
You want to hump
Something
Anything
And you want the hump to go on forever
To never stop
To blow fast
To last
This great effort, this
Sexy hump

But your bed's empty
And you're all alone
And your hand looks at you
You swear it's giving you the eye

So you smile back

Only Half

Why are so many poems about death?
she asked me.

Coz that's half of the big deal
I replied. So,

you've got to dedicate *some*
to that half.

What about the other half?
she asked.

Ah, no one wants to hear
about *that* one.

I do, she said.

Okay then. When?

Well, not yet.
Maybe later.

See?

The Sleeper

he stalked thru the world
feeling the flowers as he ran

every time he lost it
it was usually found under his bed

in the evening as the sun went down
he looked up

the birds were melting in the trees

Love Story

We drink
we fuck
we try
to get it
right
and sometimes
I say
something
good and
you listen
like you
care
but then again
talk is cheap
so we open
another
bottle and
fall into
bed
where we
die and
die
again!

Square as Hell

A quarter full of happiness, the rest is debris and rusty fishhooks,
I said.
I bet you're a half-empty bloke, she laughed.
I ignored her and focused on my square Jack Daniel's whisky glass.
There was one corner that tasted like hell when I supped from it.
I knew that was where the bad spirits dwelled, where they
smiled up at me as my face danced blind in the heat.
And they judged me, they all judged me, every single last one of them.
And somewhere I could hear a blues master growling swampy
black lyrics and rattling his acoustic guitar with a touch of slide,
so I smiled for no other reason than
to show this sadness I meant business.

And the Birds Burn into the Sun

The sky's a pink colouration
Silhouettes of trees
TV aerials
Black shapes stabbing out

And in the distance
Rushhour traffic hissing homeward
Even the birds are lost

'But I heart you' you say 'and
isn't that enough?'
I don't reply

Sunsets don't scare me
The dream is all I'm after

Poem You

This poem was written on your back
while you were sleeping,
straight onto your dreaming flesh.

As if balanced there, kissing your pale skin,
it didn't say much, just a note to you,
just a thought:

that I wanted to wrap you up in a poem,
to blanket you in some words,
to keep you cosy in the morning sunlight.

And I didn't know if you'd see them
as you got up to get ready for work,
maybe just wash them straight off

down the plughole without noticing.
Then I heard you in the bathroom say:
'Hey! What've you written on me?'

And I smiled to myself:
just words
on your body.

The Bluest Blues

Listen to the
blueness there's
nothing left but
this blue haze
everywhere this
blue haze in
blue air this
blue room
in which I sit
feeling the blue
come down
around me
over everything
envelops
blows blue
sad empty
like there's
no other
kind of
colour

Send these Poems to Hell

My poems are tough, tougher than me.
My poems are tough guys.

They're dirtier too, meaner, than I am,
Than I can ever hope to be.

They're blunt, ruthless things. Vicious and
Unwelcome. Hard and bitter.

And they get away with it, what they want.
They get away with it all, but that's okay.

They have a right, so I leave them alone.
I let them do as they please.

What can I do? It's just me and them.
It's just us in here.

My poems are mean bastards
But they're good to me.

So I hide behind them, I hold them against
The world.

Just admit defeat: if your poems are tough
You'll never get free.

The only thing you can do
Is endure.

Our Poems

Our poems make love
Coz we do not

Our poems walk the streets
Looking for a place to go

They meet up secretly
And check into seedy hotels
On the edge of town
And fuck it all away
Till there's nothing left
No day and no night

Our poems are lovers
We are not

But our poems always
Tell it
Better than we could
Ever hope to

They always seem
To get it
Right
As we hang our heads
And sneer

Our poems are lovers
Or fuckers
But not strangers

Not like us

Our poems will last
Coz we will not

They have a right to
Exist and
Be happy

I guess we're
Just not there yet

Stirring Through Thoughts That Mean Absolutely Nothing

Pissing into a wine bottle
At 3am
And outside there are
Things
I will never care about:
Howling streets
Puked kebabs
Pissed-up doorways
Hungry taxis
Staggering heels
Dirty fucks in dirty alleys
And good old cans
Rattling in the gutters
On through the night
The hard bone moon
A flashing blade
Smiling in the dark
We are all out there
Like we are all in here
Finding new ways to live
Old ways die
Mostly they are the same
But at times
Like this
We can do neither
As I get back into bed
Pull up the sheets
The shadows come too

And you stir
You stir
My god
How you stir

Black Wine

The nights burn everything in their path
everything they touch
and have no end

And this black wine
has been
killing us for days

'Oh you fucking love it'
she said

I nodded and pulled down
the walls
the room
the sky

So we were done
with the world

You are not Humphrey Bogart, and you'll never get over it

Locking yourself away
in a room
with a bottle
can be as good as
locking yourself away
with a woman

Sometimes it's the same
Often it's better

Sitting there alone
watching Bogart play the classic loner
cool hard and
tough
straight
the main guy
the way you long to be

It's at these times
in these rooms where
everything can be good
a little while longer
can be good
at last

As if everything was
black and
white

but
with no
white

and all the
black
in the
world

K.O.C.

High as a kite or
low as a cunt,

it's the in-between
that makes life so hard to live.

Pollock

stick in the sky
what's that stick?
held
flicked
paint splattered
dripped?

and the man
possessed
bent
over
round all 4 sides
the mad canvass

stick flung
colours spread
cross
mean something
say anything

no question
no answer
never was

just technique
spontaneous
technique

art reaching its
final destination

Your Red

I really loved it there in your red room,
Where we drank cheap wine
And searched for cigarettes and Rizla,
Where we decided the rest of the world
Was not red enough
For us.

Long days in that place where you told me
Charles Bukowski was Charles Baudelaire
Reincarnated, and that it was 'sooo obvious.'
'Well, who am I?' I asked.
'Jane Austen,' you replied.
'I always thought so,' I said.

And your rocking chair where I sat
And read ancient magazines you never threw away,
Listening to your terrible CD collection
Or watching films you owned but had never seen.
You chatted the whole way through them each time
Leaving me to know all the words.

If heaven was white and the sky was blue,
The world some other shade I
Couldn't even fathom or make out,
And the colours of other girls' rooms
Were less important,
It all didn't matter to me.

It was only your room,
Only deep in that red,
Some place
That could've
Represented
Your heart.

Ask My Dick

In the past and I knew it was
Love
Coz you didn't have to rub
My dick it
Came to meet you when you
Walked in the door

And I just lay back with
This jutting obelisk
(I wish!)
In the sky in
Your hungry blue eyes

You wanted it and
It seemed to want you back
I was too uninvolved and
Underestimated to care

You two had each other
And that was enough

It was love it was love
It was sex it was sex
It was love I
Swear it was

Coz a hard dick can't lie
Not that it don't want to

The End of a Love

Don't abandon my ancient love,
my red heart,
my red nose.
Adore my passion,
my amour
hiding in heavy armour,
hanging in the armoire.

Just tie down my old memories
of the time.
I can remember all the things she told me:

that first girl.

'You awake?' she asked me.

'What's wrong?' I said.

'I'd rather do it all and die,
    than to die unhappy.'

'You'll get what you deserve.'

'I hope so.'

We kissed.

And who knew endings were this still?

Interrogation whilst eating a Cherry in the World

I am eating a cherry and watching your toes wriggle on the carpet,
the sunlight tickling them, making them curl and seem to laugh,
cute pink babies with red toenail faces,

and you look at me with absinthe eyes from a dream and say,
'What are you thinking?'

I spit out my pip into the ashtray and reply,
'I can't remember.'

I never know the answer to that one.

You've Been Back Here, I Can Tell

Lock the door and
don't come back
I mean it
I *try* to mean it

But I know you've been here
I know you have
when I was out
of my mind

You've been in through
the window again and
left your muddy marks
on the kitchen top

Your high heels
scuffed the surface
but it's okay
this time

The surface is not me or
anything like me
But I won't say it doesn't hurt
I won't say that

Varnish

The end of the
world
as she paints her
finger
nail

Pink
soft
pink

And she
blows
shakes and
dips
starts the next
one
until all five
are
complete

And the rest of
us
never
existed
at
all

Indentation of Something

Add to the darkness
the long stirring,
the bitter landscape.

Add the screaming rain.
Everything learns
to twist in the dust.

Don't look back
or ahead,
concentrate
on your feet,
think:
are my shoes big enough?
are my balls?
am I prepared
for what's going down here?

Drinking will soften the blow,
it will make it
not so tough.

This is the world and you have
to make an impression,
leave an imprint,
a dent,
an outline
of something.

You have to change
everything
a little

if it’s worth it,
if
anything is.

I am eating an apple

I am eating an apple
As the world turns
And men and women kill each other

I am eating an apple
At the start of the century
As dogs chase sticks
And wars are being fought somewhere else

I am eating an apple
In a civilisation I cannot explain
In a society that is strange

But I am eating an apple
Like a deadly art
Or an ancient myth
Or a cult
Where only the snakes are not scared

This Sober Thing

Sobriety's like death
a little bit and
these cups of tea
just don't get me
anywhere!

I'm on the wagon,
but I hope
the wheels come off!

Do Another Day

Night. Strange blue coming in,
my wild head eating up thoughts,
the clock's noose around my neck.

And there's a large number of sheep in this tomb,
about 2 per second,
for hours now.

There's a thick panic when I discover birdsong:
it's early it's late,
it's morning it's night.

Perhaps a drink will soften the blow
as the quick hours fall
away into the dawn.

Get up and get to work, sad life,
know the poet's
the lowest paid creature in humanity.

But still, as an alligator caked in cool mud,
eyes flicker
at the thought of the world.

With an alarming sound I get up,
into the universe.
I drift into the sun,

where I harden,
ripen,
and burn.

For You, Babe

The days burn
almost as much
as the nights
ever did
and yes you're still a
blonde maniac

but your tits are good
and your arse is good
and your pussy is
very good

and I love that
small roll of fat
over your jeans
or the way you
spit out your gum or
smoke half a cigarette
or belch
just like a man

It's these little things that
numb the heavy burn
that almost heal
this pain

like it's only temporary
of course

like you
like me
like this

moment

right now
going
out

of our minds

Boil

In the end we
all boil down
to absolute nothing
and life claims back
the space
in which we hung.

Vow

I'm not drinking
any
more

but

I'm not drinking
any
less

As I Do My Best

The walls are burning down
as I sit
thinking of something
to think about.

There is no sky in here
with me.

I want you to know
how hard this is
to do, how
hard it is when
your thoughts
must get scribbled down
and typed
and filed
in some kind of order,
for no other reason
than to satisfy your own madness.

And even though
nothing changes,
it's necessary,
it's all consuming,
it's vital in itself.

The words need to feel
like I'm doing my best
for them

and
I have to feel
I'm doing my part:
keeping madness at bay
that little bit longer.

So I keep on.
So I don't stop.
So would you.
So would you.

But will it always be this way

Forming

A tall bottle,
a glass,
a room with
me inside it.

Forming the poem,
working it out,
pouring it slow,
making it.
Just letting it all
come now.

The wine makes
everything
easy.

Just me and this
precious thing
bubbling up
to the surface.

And sometimes
there's a girl.
Sometimes she's
in here
with me.

Sometimes she's
enough,
she's the poem.

But sometimes
she's not
and
sometimes
nothing
is true…

Through Walls

There's sunlight on the carpet,
Coming from the window,
The world outside,
Thick rich shafts,
And we listen,
Not to the sunlight,
As that doesn't make a sound,
But to next door
Killing themselves again:
Through the walls
The awful fight,
Vicious words
Spat, hissed, thrown,
Slamming doors, drawers
(Knocks the morning
Off its hinges).
'I hope we don't end up like that,'
She says to me.
I don't reply.
We just sit,
Our sad cheeks resting
On the arms of the chairs
Like limp dead fish,
And there's sunlight on the carpet.

Love Is Just Another Arsehole

Love is just an arsehole,
a space in the dark.

You didn't realise, but
when you left
you thought you took
my heart
but
you actually took
my arsehole.

You see, I swapped them
sometime in the night
when you weren't
looking,
when I knew you
were going to break
everything.

So, you can't hurt my heart.

You can try to hurt
my arsehole, but
you and I both know
that arseholes are
tough
and don't break
easily.

Better luck next time
darling, and
I mean all this
from the
heart
of my
bottom.

Try This

There's no more jokes
about your face, about
your weight or your
inky eyes.

There's no more light
on us, on where we
used to be, the place
we used to exist.

Our miracles are dumb and
only for us. You see we
don't perform much
anymore.

But use your oils,
paint sunflowers,
cut off an ear and
give it to me.

Has that been done
before? I was only
trying to be
romantic.

Maybe just wrap your lips
around my life and
think of something
good to say.

Think of something
good.

www.ingramcontent.com/pod-product-compliance
Lightning Source LLC
Chambersburg PA
CBHW022201160726
48282CB00024B/280
9788119654512